CONTENTS

©2013, from *String Quilts with Style* (AQS, 1999)

Bobbie A. Aug

Sharon Newman

ABOUT THE AUTHORS

Bobbie Aug and the late Sharon Newman met in Paducah, Kentucky, at the 1989 American Quilter's Society Show. Both learned to sew on treadle sewing machines, Bobbie in Illinois and Sharon in Indiana. Their love and appreciation of quilts brought them together.

Sharon's interest in quiltmaking began in Indiana as the granddaughter of a prolific quiltmaker. Sharon focused on quilts and quiltmaking and participation in the Texas Quilt Search. She wrote seven books on quiltmaking and quilt history, and she was nationally recognized for her reproduction fabric lines from Moda Fabrics.

Bobbie Aug was inspired by the quiet, dignified beauty of nineteenth-century quilts and began making quilts more than 40 years ago. She became a quilt dealer, quilt collector, quilt shop owner, and quilt show consultant and producer, focusing on anything related to quilts and quiltmaking.

BASIC STRING PIECING

As the term is used here, a "string" is a long narrow strip of fabric. Strings can be any length and can vary in width. In this book, they range from ½" to 4" wide, but most average about 1"–1½" wide. The strings need not be even or symmetrical, since the beauty of the technique is in the asymmetrical appearance.

Strings are sewn to a paper or fabric foundation to provide a temporary base for the pattern pieces. Paper foundations are removed before the quilt is layered with batting and backing. Fabric foundations are left in place, making the finished piece heavier and more difficult to hand quilt. Therefore, fabric-foundation quilts can be machine quilted or tied. We have chosen to use paper foundations for all the quilts in this book. Any thin, lightweight paper will do. Tissue paper and parchment paper are good choices and are easy to remove. Other possibilities include tracing paper, freezer paper, or thin typing paper.

MAKING TEMPLATES

Some patches in the quilts may require making templates. For convenience, use clear plastic acetate to make them. The type of acetate marked with a grid makes it easy to cut true 90° angles and to line up the grain of the fabrics you will be cutting. Cut templates for machine stitching with the ¼" seam allowance included. With a fine, permanent marker, carefully trace each different shape to be used in a pattern on template material and cut out carefully along the marked lines. When tracing patterns for templates, be sure to include the arrows for aligning the patterns with the fabric grain. Use templates to mark fabric on the wrong side, keeping a sharp pencil or chalk point as close to the template edges as possible. A 0.5mm mechanical pencil is useful for marking all but the darkest of fabrics, for which you can use a white pencil. Cut the fabric along the marked lines.

PLANNING FABRICS AND COLORS

Choose 100% cotton scraps for ease in sewing the string-pieced units. Mix plaids, solids, stripes, and prints. While each set of directions suggests an approximate total amount of fabric for strings, you will need to determine specific amounts for each fabric. Be sure to have enough of any colors that predominate, repeat, or act as an accent. Since you will be making fabric choices as you string-piece, it's a good idea to plan for extra fabric so you can have complete freedom of choice as you work.

Before you begin to sew, sort your fabrics by color. Within each color, divide your scraps into light, medium, and dark. Consider the balance of your fabrics. You may find you need to add a few lights or darks.

Viewing actual fabrics alongside each other is the best way to reach a satisfying combination for your quilt. However, if the color photograph of the quilt you want to make limits your imagination, you can photocopy the assembly diagram on a black and white copier and use markers or colored pencils to audition other possibilities.

Prewash all the fabrics you have chosen. Washing them removes the final finishing products and shrinks the fabrics. You can wash in color groups, but watch the process to see if you have dye loss in the first water. For best results, press the fabrics while they are still slightly damp.

A "string" is a long, narrow strip of fabric.

STRING-PIECING TECHNIQUE

To begin a string-pieced quilt, decide on the basic shape to be used for the string-pieced portion. Squares, rectangles, triangles, and diamonds – the basic shapes of many patchwork patterns – are popular for string-pieced quilt designs. Cut pieces of paper or fabric in that shape for the foundations. For a large quilt, cut long strings across the full width of the fabric. Cut at a slight angle, so that the strings are wider at one end.

Cut a length of string so that it will extend at least ½" beyond the edges of the paper foundation. Place it across the paper near the center (Figure 1–1). Cut and place a second string from a different fabric on the first string, with right sides together and one long edge aligned. Sew the strings together on the aligned edge (Figure 1–2) with a ¼" seam allowance all the way to the end plus ½" beyond the paper.. Lift the top string and press (Figure 1–3). In the same way, sew a string to the opposite side of the center string. Continue adding strings on both sides of the center string, pressing after each addition. Trim the ends of the strings ¼" away from the edges of the paper foundation (Figure 1–4) so the paper is not caught in the seam when joining blocks.

By chain piecing strings, you can reduce the number of steps to the ironing board. Put your ironing board at your elbow to save even more steps. Steam press, making sure the right side is smooth with no little fold at the seam line.

It is important that all seams lie flat and smooth in string-pieced shapes. After each string is sewn, press the seam allowance just sewn to set the seam. Lift up the top strip and press the piece on the right side. Each string should be pressed before another is sewn to it.

Leave paper foundations in place until the quilt top has been completed. This provides stability for the many bias areas and multiple seam lines inherent in the technique and prevents stretching and distortion.

The small stitches, used to sew the strings, perforate the paper. To remove the foundation, you can use a tool, such as a seam ripper, to score the paper along the seam lines and make an opening in the paper. Pull the paper against the seam lines and it will separate along the stitching. The tool can also help you lift sections of paper easily.

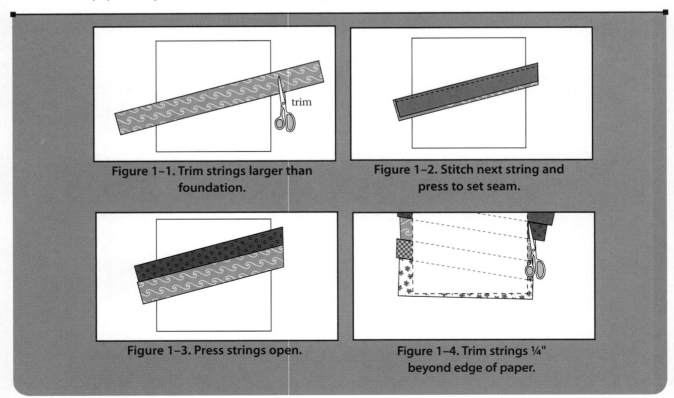

Figure 1–1. Trim strings larger than foundation.

Figure 1–2. Stitch next string and press to set seam.

Figure 1–3. Press strings open.

Figure 1–4. Trim strings ¼" beyond edge of paper.

  Bobbie A. Aug & Sharon Newman

TAPESTRY

Quilt size 44" x 62"

Finished string-pieced rectangle 6" x 9"

CUTTING REQUIREMENTS

PAPER FOUNDATIONS

36 rectangles 6½" x 9½"

SCRAPS 2 yds. equivalent

Strings average 2½" wide

ACCENT FABRIC 1⅛ yds.

Center strings average 2½" wide

5 border insert strips 1½" wide, cut selvage to selvage

MITERED BORDER 2 yds.

2 strips 4½" x 64½"

2 strips 4½" x 46½"

BINDING ¾ yd.

Cut 2"-wide bias strips from 24" square

BACKING 4 yds.

2 panels 24½" x 66"

BATTING 48" x 66"

TAPESTRY, by Bobbie Aug; machine quilted by Janet Spencer.

Rectangles of strings placed on the diagonal are joined in groups of four to create abstract diamonds. The pink strings laid down the center of each block give continuity to the design.

Bobbie A. Aug & Sharon Newman

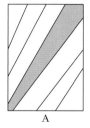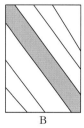

A   B

Figure 2–1. String-pieced rectangles.

SEWING DIRECTIONS

1 MAKE STRING-PIECED RECTANGLES: Arrange the strings diagonally across each foundation, starting with the accent color in the center. Make 18 A rectangles and 18 B rectangles as shown in Figure 2–1. Sew strings ½" beyond the paper edges. Trim the strings ¼" away from the edges of the paper. This way the paper is not caught in the seams when joining blocks.

2 ARRANGE RECTANGLES: Arrange the string-pieced rectangles side by side in 6 rows of 6, alternating rectangles A and B to create the design (see Quilt Assembly diagram). Note that the accent strings emphasize the diamond formation created by grouping rectangles.

3 ASSEMBLE QUILT TOP: Join the rectangles in each row. Press seam allowances one direction in odd-numbered rows and the opposite direction in even-numbered rows. Taking care to match the seams and easing any slight fullness, join the rows. Press all the seam allowances in the same direction between rows.

4 ADD BORDER INSERT: Measure the length and width of the quilt across the center to determine the exact lengths needed for the border inserts. Sew the 5 border insert strips together to make the lengths needed. Sew the insert strips to the quilt.

5 ATTACH BORDERS: Matching half and quarter measurements, pin and sew a 64½" border strip to each side of the quilt and a 46½" strip to the top and bottom. (As you sew, you will catch the border insert in the seams.) Miter the border corners. Press the seam allowances open at the miters and press all others toward the borders. Remove paper foundations.

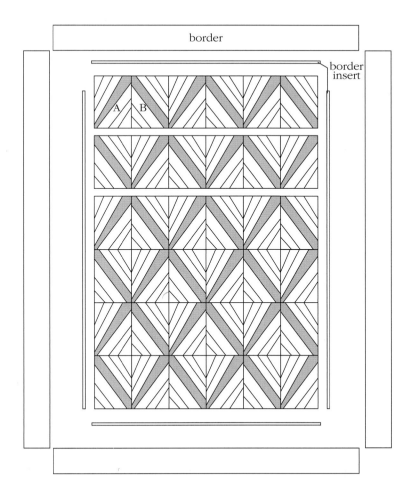

Quilt Assembly

6 **MARK QUILTING:** Mark the quilting design on the quilt top (see Quilting Design below). To use the full-size quilting pattern on page 9, trace the design from the book onto tracing paper. Then, using a source of backlighting, trace the design on your fabric. Frame each floral quilting motif with quilted diamonds by quilting down the center of each string. Mark the borders in parallel diagonal lines approximately 2" apart, starting at the center of each side and working outward.

7 **FINISH QUILT:** Layer the quilt top, batting, and backing. Baste the layers together. After quilting by hand or machine, remove the basting and trim the batting and backing even with the quilt top. Finish the edges with 2"-wide bias binding. Add a sleeve in the back for hanging the quilt, if desired. Remember to sign and date your quilt.

Quilting Design (top left corner)

TAPESTRY
Full-Size Quilting Pattern

Bobbie A. Aug & Sharon Newman

CUTTING REQUIREMENTS

PAPER FOUNDATIONS

90 rectangles 4" x 8"

SCRAPS 3½ yds. equivalent

Strings average 2" wide

SASHES, BORDERS, AND BINDING 4½ yds.

10 sashes 4" x 77½", cut parallel to selvages

2 border strips 4" x 69", cut parallel to selvages

Binding, cut 2"-wide bias strips from 27" square

BACKING 5 yds.

2 panels 36" x 86"

BATTING 70½" x 86"

LOOSE CHANGE, by Bobbie Aug; machine quilted by Janet Spencer.

The bar setting gave this quilt its structure since all the fabric pieces were selected and sewn at random. This design is a variation of the classic Chinese Coins pattern. Perhaps the green sashing and border fabric calls paper money to mind.

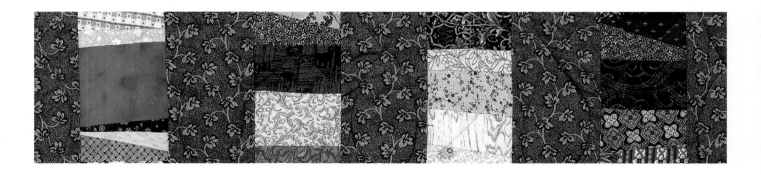

SEWING DIRECTIONS

1 **MAKE STRING-PIECED RECTANGLES:** Sew strings crosswise on the foundation rectangles ending ½" beyond the foundation edges. After you have filled the foundations with strings, trim them ¼" away from the edges of the paper so that the paper will not be caught in the seams when joining blocks.

2 **SEW RECTANGLES INTO STRIPS:** Sew the string-pieced rectangles together in 9 vertical strips of 10 rectangles each. Press the seam allowances downward in each row.

3 **MEASURE ROWS:** The string-pieced strips need to be within ¼" of each other in length. If the discrepancy is greater than ¼", adjust the strips by taking in or letting out the seam allowances between the rectangles. Then determine the average length of the strips.

4 **TRIM SASHING STRIPS:** The 10 sashes need to be trimmed to the average length of the string-pieced strips. Mark the half, quarter, and eighth measurements on all strips.

5 **ASSEMBLE QUILT TOP:** Starting and ending with a sash, alternate sashes and string-pieced strips (refer to the Quilt Assembly diagram). Pin and sew the strips together, matching the half, quarter, and eighth measurements. Add the border strips to the top and bottom of the quilt. Trim the border strips even with the quilt edges and remove the paper foundations.

6 **MARK QUILTING DESIGN:** It is generally easier to mark the quilt top before the quilt is layered. In this quilt, the borders and sashing strips have been quilted in a curved cable pattern. The string-pieced rows have been quilted in an angular cable design.

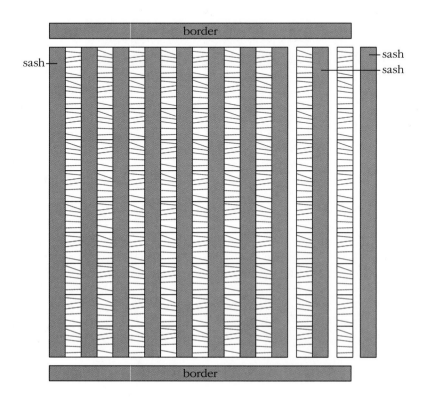

7 FINISH QUILT: Layer the quilt top, batting, and backing and baste the layers together. After quilting by hand or machine, remove the basting and trim the batting and backing even with the quilt top. Finish the edges with 2"-wide bias binding. Add a sleeve in the back for hanging the quilt, if desired. Remember to sign and date your quilt.

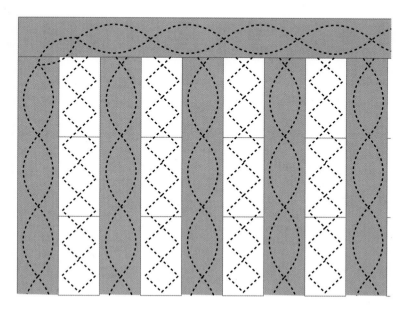

Quilting Design (top left corner)

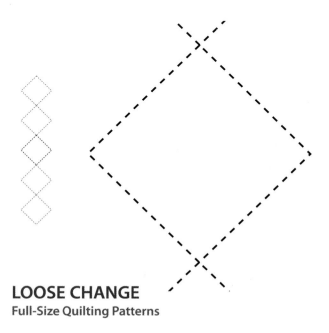

LOOSE CHANGE
Full-Size Quilting Patterns

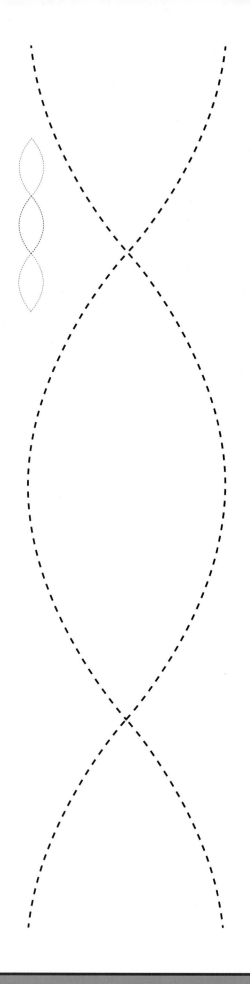

DOUBLE CROSS

Quilt size 52½" x 69"
Finished string-pieced square 5¾"
Finished block 13½"

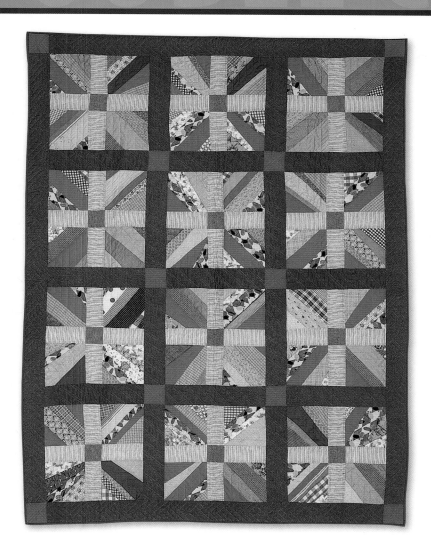

CUTTING REQUIREMENTS

PAPER FOUNDATIONS

48 squares 6¼"

SCRAPS 2⅜ yds. equivalent

Strings average 2¼" wide

BLUE PRINT 2 yds.

2 border strips 3½" x 65½",
cut parallel to selvages

2 border strips 3½" x 49",
cut parallel to selvages

17 sashes 3½" x 14"

TAN STRIPE ¾ yd.

48 sashes 2½" x 6¼"

ORANGE SOLID ¼ yd.

10 setting squares 3½"

ORANGE PRINT ¼ yd.

12 setting squares 2½"

BINDING ¾ yd.

Cut 2"-wide bias strips from 25" square

BACKING 4⅜ yds.

2 panels 29" x 73"

BATTING 56½" x 73"

DOUBLE CROSS, by Terri Ellis.

To show that string quilting is not new, the four square units in each block in this quilt were pieced on newspaper from around 1940. The tan sashing within each block and the blue sashing that sets the blocks were chosen to enhance the original colors. This technique of double sashing is used effectively in many patterns that include small blocks.

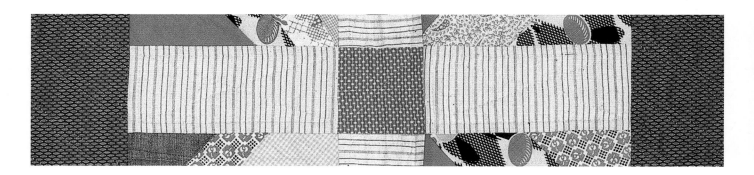

SEWING DIRECTIONS

1 **MAKE STRING-PIECED SQUARES:** Sew the strings on the diagonal ½" beyond the edges of the paper. Use an orange accent in a majority of the squares. Trim the strings ¼" away from the edges of the paper foundations so that the paper is not caught in the seams when joining blocks.

2 **SEW BLOCKS:** Refer to the Block Assembly diagram and make 12 blocks, each containing 4 string-pieced squares, 4 tan stripe sashes, and 1 orange-print setting square. Be sure to check the orientation of the diagonal strings as you sew. Press seam allowances toward the sashes.

3 **ASSEMBLE QUILT TOP:** Arrange quilt blocks in 4 rows of 3. Sew 3½" x 14" blue sashes between the three blocks in each row (see Quilt Assembly diagram). Join 3 sashes alternately with 2 orange setting squares to make a sashing row. Make 3 rows in this manner. Sew the sashing rows in between the block rows.

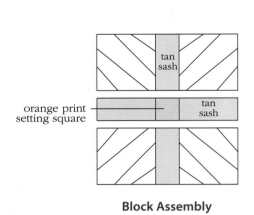

Block Assembly

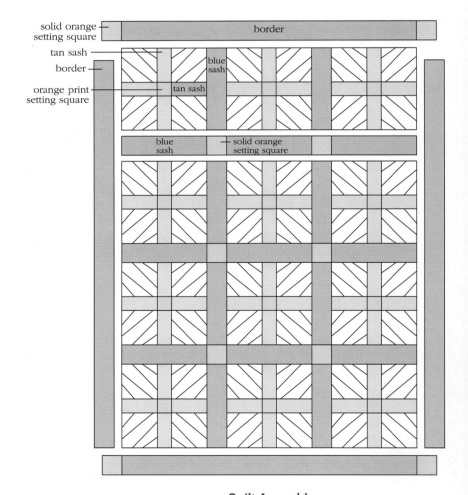

Quilt Assembly

4 ADD BORDERS: Mark half and quarter measurements. Before adding the long side borders, measure the quilt width and trim the top and bottom borders to this measurement. Set them aside. Stitch the long border strips to the sides of the quilt. Trim the strips even with the quilt edges. Stitch the orange setting squares to the ends of the top and bottom border strips and sew them to the quilt. Remove paper foundations.

5 MARK QUILTING DESIGN: It is generally easier to mark the quilt top before the quilt is layered. Use a ruler to mark the various patterns shown in the Quilting Design diagram below, or quilt as desired.

6 FINISH QUILT: Layer the quilt top, batting, and backing. Pin or thread baste the layers together. After quilting the design, remove the basting and trim the batting and backing even with the quilt top. Bind your quilt with 2"-wide bias binding. Remember to sign and date your quilt.

Quilting Design (top left corner)

Bobbie A. Aug & Sharon Newman

FESTIVAL
Quilt size 47½" x 57½"

CUTTING REQUIREMENTS

PAPER FOUNDATIONS

36 half-square triangles cut from 18 squares 8"

SCRAPS 1½ yds. equivalent

Strings average 2¾" wide

BLACK 3⅛ yds.

36 side triangles, cut from 9 squares 11½"

16 corner triangles, cut from 8 squares 6"

2 border strips 4" x 53"

2 border strips 4" x 50"

Binding, cut 2"-wide bias strips from 23" square

BACKING 3⅝ yds.

2 panels 26½" x 61½"

BATTING 51½" x 61½"

FESTIVAL, by Bobbie Aug; machine quilted by Janet Spencer.

Sharp zigzags of a classic Streak o' Lightning pattern always seem more complex than they really are, and the string-pieced triangles add to the amazing effects. Rich, bright colors set against a black background make this quilt visually exciting.

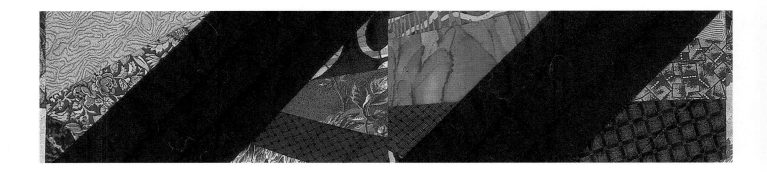

SEWING DIRECTIONS

1 MAKE STRING-PIECED TRIANGLES: Sew the strings more or less perpendicular to the base of the triangle extending the stitches to ½" beyond the paper edges. Trim the strings ¼" away from the edges of the paper foundations to keep the paper from being caught in the seams when joining blocks.

2 CUT BACKGROUND TRIANGLES: Cut the 11½" squares in half diagonally twice (Figure 2–7) to make the 36 side triangles. Cut the 6" squares in half diagonally once (Figure 2–8) to make the 16 corner triangles.

3 ASSEMBLE QUILT TOP: Sew the string-pieced and side triangles in vertical strips as shown in the Quilt Assembly diagram. Add the corner triangles to square off each strip. Please note: For ease in measuring and assembly, the side and corner triangles were cut slightly oversized. Trim each pieced strip, leaving ¼" seam allowances beyond the points all around. Sew the strips together.

4 ADD BORDERS: Matching half and quarter measurements, sew the long border strips to the sides and trim any extra length even with the quilt edges. In the same manner, add borders to the top and bottom. Remove paper foundations.

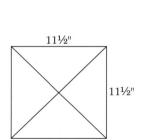

11½"

11½"

Figure 2–7.
Cut 4 side triangles from each square.

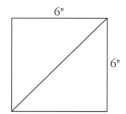

6"

6"

Figure 2–8.
Cut 2 corner triangles from each square.

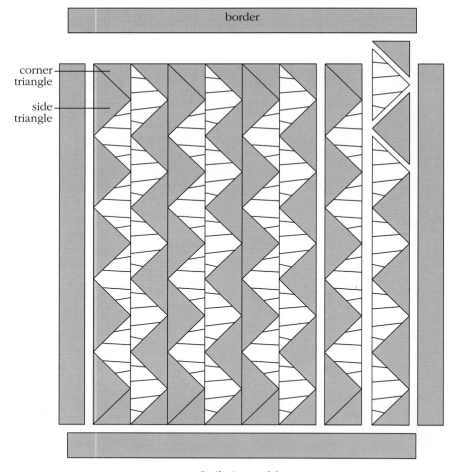

border

corner triangle

side triangle

Quilt Assembly

5 MARK QUILTING: It is generally easier to mark the quilt top before the quilt is layered. As shown, the quilting pattern echoes the zigzag lines of the patchwork. Mark the strips and extend the parallel lines into the border. Refer to the Quilting Design diagram.

6 FINISH QUILT: Layer the quilt top, batting, and backing. Baste the layers together. After quilting the design, remove the basting and trim the batting and backing even with the quilt top. Bind the quilt with 2"-wide bias binding. Remember to sign and date your quilt.

Quilting Design (top left corner)

Bobbie A. Aug & Sharon Newman

CUTTING REQUIREMENTS

PAPER FOUNDATIONS

15 squares 4"

SCRAPS ½ yd. equivalent

Strings average 1½" wide

BACKGROUND ⅜ yd.

24 side triangles, cut from 6
squares 6¼"

12 corner triangles, cut from 6
squares 3½"

PLAID 1 yd.

4 vertical sashes 2¾" x 27½"

Binding, cut 2"-wide bias strips
from 17" square

BACKING ⅞ yd.

1 panel 28" x 29"

BATTING 28" x 29"

SQUARED STRINGS II, by Gwen Davis Oberg. The country folk-art look of this small quilt is the result of combining beige, red, and green plaids. Because the strings are skewed, the plaids also seem skewed. Combined with the on-point setting, this fresh and lively quilt is full of visual movement. The hand quilting adds plenty of charm.

SEWING DIRECTIONS

1 **MAKE STRING-PIECED SQUARES:** Sew the strings diagonally across each foundation square, sewing ½" beyond the edges of the paper. Trim the strings ¼" away from the edges of the paper to keep the paper from being caught in the seams when joining blocks.

2 **CUT BACKGROUND TRIANGLES:** Cut the 6½" squares diagonally twice (Figure 2–9) to make the 24 side triangles. Cut the 3½" squares in half diagonally (Figure 2–10) to make the 12 corner triangles.

3 **MAKE PIECED VERTICAL STRIPS:** Assemble the string-pieced squares and background triangles in 3 vertical strips of 5 squares each, as shown in the Quilt Assembly diagram. Sew the squares and triangles in diagonal rows, then sew the rows together to complete the strips. Please note: For ease in measuring and assembly, the triangles were cut slightly oversized. Trim each pieced strip, leaving ¼" seam allowances beyond the points all around.

4 **TRIM VERTICAL SASHES:** Measure the string-pieced strips. They should be within ⅛" of each other. If they are not, you can make adjustments in the seams between the rows. Trim the sashes to match the pieced strips in length.

5 **ASSEMBLE QUILT TOP:** To keep the string-pieced squares aligned across the quilt, mark the following placement guides on the long edges of the sashes. Place the first mark 2½" from the top, then place four marks at 5" intervals (see Figure 2–11). Match these marks to the square points in the string-pieced strips, then pin. (Sew with the pieced strips on top so you can see the points.) Remove paper foundations.

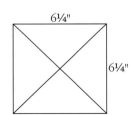

6¼"

6¼"

Figure 2–9.
Cut 4 side triangles from each square.

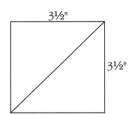

3½"

3½"

Figure 2–10.
Cut 2 corner triangles from each square.

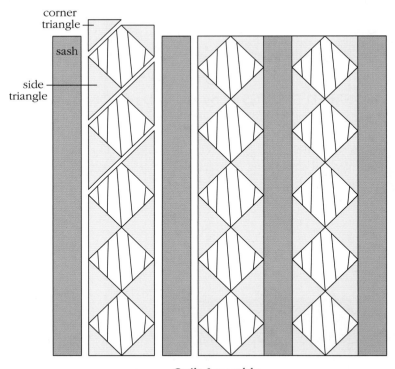

corner triangle

sash

side triangle

Quilt Assembly

6 **MARK QUILTING:** Mark the quilting design, if desired, before layering the quilt top, batting, and backing. A simple square within a square pattern was quilted across the sashing strips between the string-pieced squares.

7 **FINISH QUILT:** Layer the top, batting, and backing, and baste the layers together. Stitch in the ditch around each string block and quilt along the marked lines, or as desired. Remove the basting and trim the batting and backing even with the quilt top. Finish the edges with 2"-wide bias binding. Remember to sign and date your quilt.

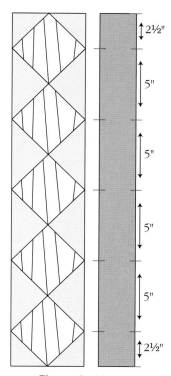

Figure 2–11.
Place matching marks on sashes.

Quilting Design (top left corner)

Bobbie A. Aug & Sharon Newman

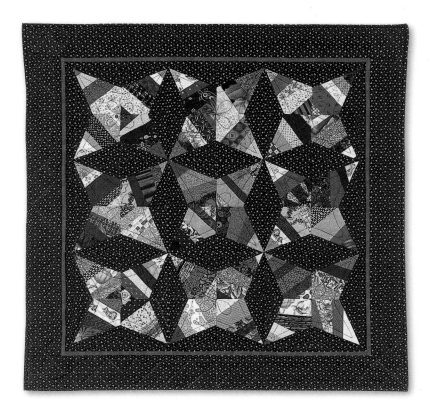

DOS STARS, by Jalinda Marlar Gieck; machine quilted by Janet Spencer.

The dark background, set against the vibrant colors of the string-pieced stars, creates a secondary star design. The inside border helps to contain the lively stars while adding excitement to the quilt.

CUTTING REQUIREMENTS

PAPER FOUNDATIONS

36 kites, pattern A

SCRAPS 1 yd. equivalent

Strings average 2" wide

ACCENT FABRIC ¼ yd.

4 border insert strips 1½" wide cut selvage to selvage

BACKGROUND 1⅝ yds.

36 B and 36 Br triangles, cut from rectangles 2⅜" x 5⅞"

2 inner borders 1½" x 30"

2 inner borders 1½" x 28"

2 outer borders 3½" x 36"

2 outer borders 3½" x 30"

Binding, cut 2"-wide bias strips from 19" square

BACKING 1⅛ yds.

1 panel 37½" square

BATTING 37½" square

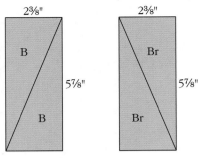

2⅜"   2⅜"

B   Br

5⅞"   5⅞"

B   Br

Figure 2–14.
Cut 18 of each.

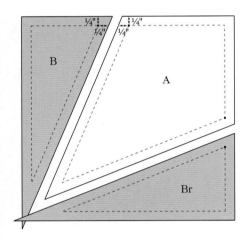

¼"   ¼"
¼"   ¼"

B

A

Br

Figure 2–15.
Mark patches as shown
to help in matching.

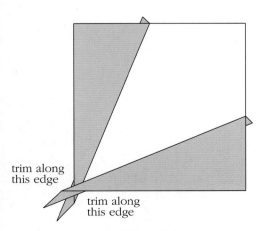

trim along
this edge

trim along
this edge

Figure 2–16.
Trim squares only
on these two sides.

SEWING DIRECTIONS

1 **MAKE STRING-PIECED KITES:** Sew the strings across the kite shapes ending ½" beyond the edges of the foundation. Trim the strings ¼" away from the edges of the paper to keep the paper from being caught in the seams when joining blocks.

2 **SEW STAR BLOCKS:** For the B patches, cut 18 of the rectangles in half along one diagonal and the other 18 rectangles on the other diagonal (Figure 2–14). To help with matching, on all A and B patches, mark the seam intersections as shown in Figure 2–15. Note: for ease of measuring and cutting, the B patches are slightly oversize. They will be trimmed after they are sewn.

Sew a B and a Br to each string-pieced kite to make a square unit. On the edges of the units adjacent to the kite points, trim the squares to 4¾" (Figure 2–16). Be careful to keep the kite units true as you trim. Sew 4 kite units together to make a star block (Figure 2–17). Make 9 star blocks.

3 **ASSEMBLE QUILT TOP:** Sew blocks in rows of 3 each, pressing the seam allowances in one direction for rows 1 and 3 and in the opposite direction for row 2. Pin the rows together, matching the seams, and stitch, easing any slight fullness. Press the seam allowances between rows all in one direction.

4 **ADD INNER BORDERS:** Matching half and quarter measurements, pin and sew a 1½" x 28" border strip to each side of the quilt. Trim the extra length even with the quilt edges. In a like manner, sew the 1½" x 30" border strips to the top and bottom. Remove paper foundations.

5 **ADD BORDER INSERT:** Measure the length and width of the quilt through the center to determine the exact lengths needed for the border inserts. Sew the 4 border insert strips together to make the lengths needed. Baste the insert strips to the quilt.

6 **ATTACH OUTER BORDERS:** Matching half and quarter measurements, sew a 3½" x 30" border strip to each side of the quilt. Trim off extra length. Then sew the 3½" x 36" border strips to the top and bottom and trim.

7 **MARK QUILTING:** It is generally easier to mark the quilt top before the quilt is layered. Refer to the Quilting Design diagram, on page 30, which shows one-quarter of the quilt. The string-pieced stars are

outline quilted and have a four-petal flower in the center. The borders feature a diamond cable design.

8 **FINISH QUILT:** Layer the quilt top, batting, and backing, and baste the layers together. After quilting the design, remove the basting and trim the batting and backing even with the quilt top. Finish the edges with 2"-wide bias binding. Remember to sign and date your quilt.

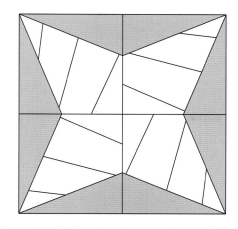

Figure 2–17. Sew 4 units to make star block.

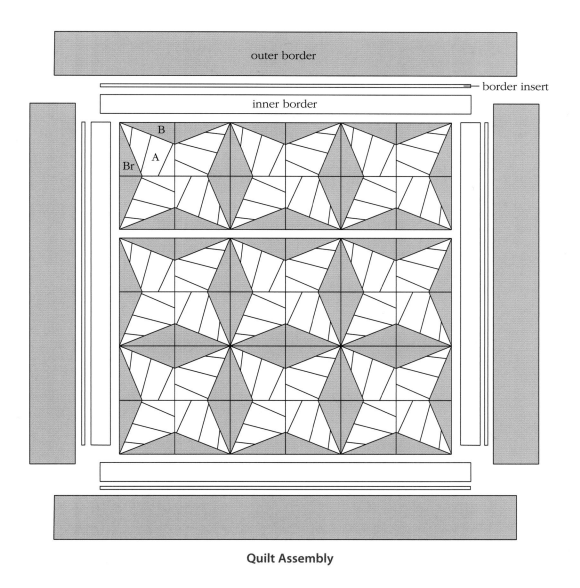

Quilt Assembly

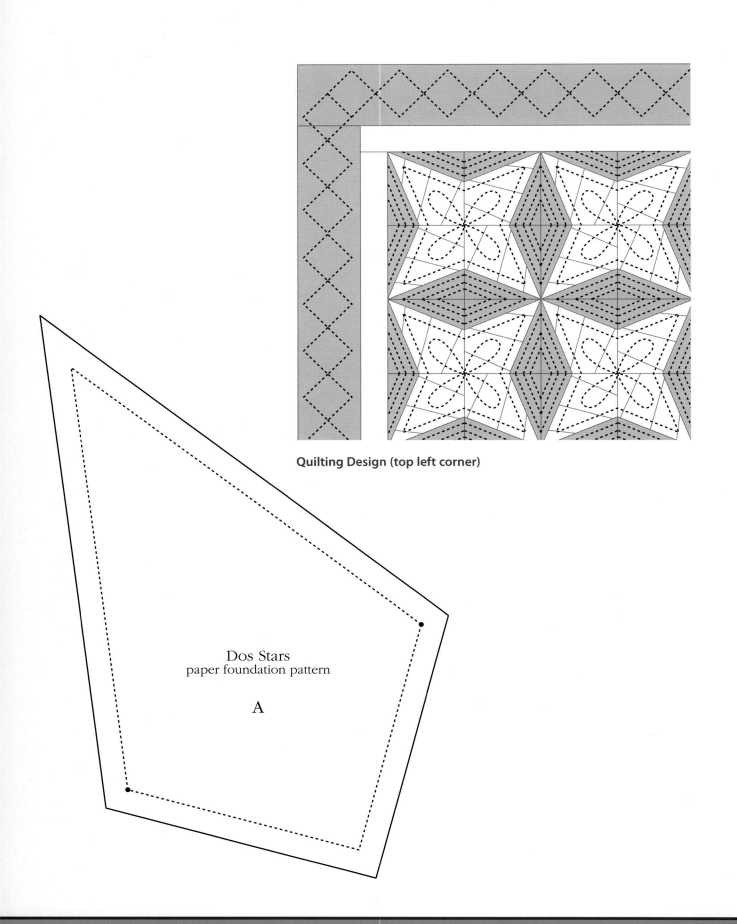

Quilting Design (top left corner)

Dos Stars
paper foundation pattern

A

Full-Size Quilting Patterns

More AQS Books

This is only a small selection of the books available from the American Quilter's Society. AQS books are known worldwide for timely topics, clear writing, beautiful color photos, and accurate illustrations and patterns. The following books are available from your local bookseller, quilt shop, or public library.

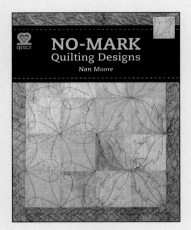

#1277

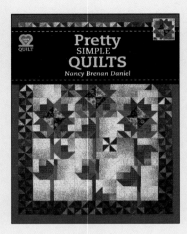

#1278

#1273

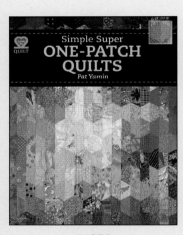

#1275

#1280

#1281

#1279

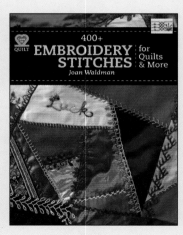

#1274

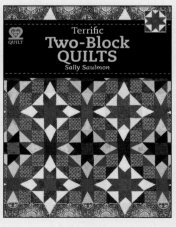

#1283